A Bird is a bird

Written by Jill Eggleton
Illustrated by Brent Chambers

PEARSON

Bird went into the tree.

"Look at me," said Bird.
"I am in my nest."

Cat went up the tree.

"Can I come in the nest?" said Cat.

Bird looked at Cat.

"No," said Bird.
"A bird is a bird
and a cat is a cat."

Cat went down the tree.
Cat went over the grass.

Bird went over
the grass, too.

Cat went into the house.

"Look at me," said Cat.
"I am in the house."

Bird went up the steps.

"Can I come
in the house?"
said Bird.

Cat looked at Bird.
"No," said Cat.
"A bird is a bird
and a cat is a cat."

A Trail

Guide Notes

Title: A Bird Is a Bird
Stage: Early (1) – Red

Genre: Fiction
Approach: Guided Reading
Processes: Thinking Critically, Exploring Language, Processing Information
Written and Visual Focus: Trail
Word Count: 108

THINKING CRITICALLY
(sample questions)
- What do you think this story could be about?
- Look at the title and read it to the children.
- How do you know Bird was showing off?
- Why do you think Bird wanted to do what Cat did?
- Why do you think Cat went into the house?
- What things could be done by both a cat and a bird?

EXPLORING LANGUAGE

Terminology
Title, cover, illustrations, author, illustrator

Vocabulary
Interest words: nest, steps, grass, tree
High-frequency words: into, looked, up, too
Positional words: up, into, over, in, down

Print Conventions
Capital letter for sentence beginnings and names (**B**ird, **C**at), full stops, commas, quotation marks, question marks